BRITAIN IN OLD PH

AROUND
ESHER

NEIL WHITE

ELMBRIDGE MUSEUM
SUTTON PUBLISHING LIMITED

Sutton Publishing Limited
Phoenix Mill · Thrupp · Stroud
Gloucestershire · GL5 2BU

First published 1996

Cover photographs: *front*: Builders erecting a
framework for a canopy at Claremont, *c.* 1900;
back: Patrons of The Swan Inn, Hare Lane,
Claygate, *c.* 1890.

British Library Cataloguing in Publication Data
A catalogue record for this book is available from the
British Library.

ISBN 0-7509-1120-4

Typeset in 10/12 Perpetua.
Typesetting and origination by
Sutton Publishing Limited.
Printed in Great Britain by
Ebenezer Baylis, Worcester.

Frontispiece: A hand-coloured print of The Tower, Esher, taken from Brayley's *History of Surrey* published in
1841. Today it is known as Wayneflete's Tower, and was built as a private house between 1478 and 1484
for Bishop William Wayneflete. It was later acquired by Henry VIII who included it in his great hunting
estate, 'The Honor of Hampton Court'. The house consisted of a huge gateway and tower, flanked on
each side by wings. Henry Pelham bought the estate in 1729, cleared away everything except the Tudor
tower, and built a new house. This in turn was later demolished leaving the remaining portion of Bishop
William's original house, which still survives today as a private residence.

Portsmouth Road, Esher, showing a gypsy encampment at the side of the road. These caravans were
grouped there for the Esher Fair which survived until 1880, when this photograph was taken.

CONTENTS

Gypsy children photographed in front of horse-drawn caravans on Arbrook Common, Esher, in 1904. Once a common sight at the turn of the century, they had disappeared from the locality by the end of the First World War.

A street party held in Park Road, Esher, to celebrate the coronation of George VI and Queen Elizabeth in May 1937. The table is laid with a good spread of food while the street has been gaily decorated with bunting.

INTRODUCTION

Esher in Old Photographs traces the changing face of a Surrey village and its environs through old photographs taken from the archives held at Elmbridge Museum. Most of the images used date from the late 1880s right up to the 1990s and are of Esher itself, as well as Claremont, West End, East and West Molesey, Hinchley Wood, Thames and Long Ditton, Weston Green and Claygate. The photographs have been arranged to take the reader on a circular tour around the area, showing some of the more interesting features of the district.

The Surrey village of Esher has a long history dating back many centuries. The village is mentioned in William the Conqueror's Domesday Survey of 1086 and, in the medieval period, Esher was home to an Augustinian Priory until the Black Death visited the area and virtually wiped out the monks. Later, Bishop Wayneflete built himself a palace over looking the River Mole on ground at Esher Place in the 1480s, which was later acquired by King Henry VIII and was included into his great deer hunting estate, called 'The Honor of Hampton Court' in the 1540s. Only the original Tudor tower now survives, as a private house.

During the eighteenth century the Esher area became the playground of the landed aristocracy, who built themselves large mansions within great estates. However, the area was still predominately rural in character, with most of the local population employed on the land, and in associated industries. However, it was the coming of the railway to Esher in 1838 that led to the development of the village and surrounding area as a residential area for the middle and working classes, a process which has continued well into the twentieth century.

Esher and the surrounding towns and villages are now part of Elmbridge Borough Council, which was created in 1974 when the old Esher Urban District Council was merged with Walton and Weybridge Urban District Council. Elmbridge was once one of fourteen Anglo-Saxons hundreds, or administrative districts, covering Surrey. The Elmbridge hundred ran from Weybridge along the river Thames to East Molesey, and southwards from the Thames to Stoke D'Abernon and incorporated most of the towns and villages featured here, except for Thames Ditton, Long Ditton and Claygate, which were situated in the Kingston hundred. The Domesday Survey of 1086 called the area Amelebridge, meaning bridge over the river Mole, or Amele as it was known in old English, was spelt Emlyn or Emley. Until the 1900s the area was called Emley Bridge.

Elmbridge Museum was created by Weybridge Urban District Council in 1909, and was known as the Weybridge Museum. In 1933 it became the museum for the Walton and Weybridge Urban District Council and in 1974 it became the local and social history museum for the new Elmbridge Borough Council. The museum collections reflect human habitation in the area from prehistoric times to the present day, with a strong emphasis on the social history of the area from the eighteenth century.

I would like to thank all the staff at Elmbridge Museum for their help in preparing this book, especially Anthea Holmes, who compiled the index. Lastly, I would like to thank my wife Sheila, and my son Jamie, for their patience while I have been writing this book.

Neil White
Elmbridge Museum
June 1996

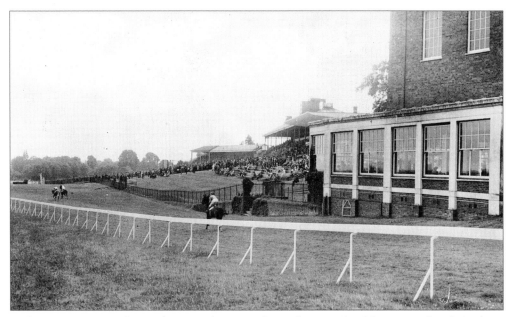

Sandown Racecourse, Esher, in the 1960s showing jockeys riding past the old main grandstand. Sandown Racecourse was rebuilt in the early 1970s.

A view of The Green, Esher, in the 1960s. The War Memorial is in the foreground, just out of the picture, and a row of eighteenth-century cottages can be seen in the distance.

ESHER

Postcard view of the Old Pump in Esher High Street in the mid-1960s. The pump shown here replaced an earlier one erected by HRH the Comte de Paris in celebration of his marriage to HRH the Infanta Marie Isabella of Spain on 30 May 1864. This view is taken from a postcard purchased by Weybridge Museum staff from Lewis and Meesons in November 1973.

The Green Banks, Esher, in the 1960s. This view shows the granite water trough and drinking fountain on the Green which was 'Presented to the Parish of Esher by Her Majesty Queen Victoria, 1877'. Behind is a statue of Britannia, by F.J. Williamson, erected in celebration of the 1897 Diamond Jubilee. The inscription on the statue reads 'Victoria Regina Et Imperatrix, 1837–1897, In commemoration of her Diamond Jubilee'. A later inscription on the side reads 'Victoria Reg et Imp. ob XXII. Jan MDCCCCI. To mark their sorrow on the death of their beloved queen and in rememberance of her residence in childhood at Claremont and of her life long interest in the village. This record is here inscribed by the people of Esher.' In the distance can be seen The Bear Hotel and public house. Surprisingly for this date, the roads are clear of traffic.

St George's Church, Esher, photographed in the 1960s from the roof of The Bear Hotel. St George's Church is built on the site of an earlier Norman church. In 1724 the Duke of Newcastle had a special pew constructed in the church in the form of a miniature aisle decorated with Corinthian columns and a pediment; this was used by the Duke of Newcastle, owner of Claremont, and his brother Henry, who lived at nearby Esher Place. With the opening of the much larger Christ Church in 1854, St George's Church fell into disuse. It is now owned by the Redundant Churches Fund and in 1990 the interior was restored; the work funded by the Friends of St George's.

A tranquil scene beside the River Mole, Esher, photographed in the mid-1960s, showing the rustic wooden footbridge in the distance.

Another view of The Bear Hotel, this time from the Green Banks, High Street, Esher, taken from a postcard issued in the 1960s. The Bear is Esher's oldest inn and dates from the fifteenth century. Its name comes from its links with the Earl of Warwick, whose coat of arms includes a bear.

An imposing view of the east window of Christ Church, Esher, in the mid-1960s. This building was designed by a pupil of Pugin, Benjamin Ferrey, and the foundation stone of the new church was laid in September 1852. Donations were the main source of income for its construction. The Bishop of Winchester consecrated the new church in 1854, and since then it has received several alterations, acquiring a new clock tower in 1868 and a new vestry in 1873. An organ was installed in 1886 and restored in 1931. In the graveyard there are two fine monuments carved by the Victorian sculptor, F.J. Williamson. One is to Lord Esher, while the other is to Arthur Doveton Clarke, his wife Edith and their son.

Moore Place Hotel, Esher, in the 1960s.

Another view of The Bear Hotel, this time dating from 1905. It shows a horse and cart parked outside and a boy standing beside the fencing near the Green. On the extreme left can be seen the Victorian drinking fountain.

A postcard view of Esher Bridge, c. 1914, from a card posted on 12 December that year. This scene shows two gentlemen, one wearing a strawboater, leaning over the stone parapet, looking down at the river.

Portsmouth Road, Esher, *c.* 1920, with two girls walking towards the camera. On the right are a pair of telegraph poles which were a common enough sight at the time of this photograph, until the lines were buried underground. A lone motor car can be seen in the distance, passing by two gas lamps. Roads at this time still had gravelled surfaces, which required constant maintenance throughout the year.

A dramatic illustration of the great fire at Burn & Co. Mills, Esher, on 14 January 1908, as depicted on a contemporary postcard. The blaze, which totally destroyed the factory, was attended by the Esher Fire Brigade, who are attempting to douse the flames with their tiny water hoses. Burn & Co. were manufacturing spiral book bindings at this mill on the banks of the River Mole from 1902. Earlier, it was used as a copper wire mill and a linoleum factory. There has been a mill at Esher since the twelfth century. The first reference to a mill is in the court rolls of King John in 1199 where it is recorded that 'the monks of St Leofride Cross came into the court of the Lord the King and entered into a recognizance to pay for their mill at Ashal (Esher) 12 broches of eels yearly to Henry de Bohun and Reginald de Cruce by the hands of Roger the Miller'. (Reproduced from *Esher: A Pictorial History* by Anthony Mitchell, Phillimore, 1995.)

A sepia photograph of Sandown House, Esher, in 1923. Sandown House stands opposite Sandown Park Racecourse and is depicted in this photograph shortly before it was purchased by Esher Urban District Council in 1923 for use as Council offices. Sandown House was built in 1740, with an adjoining park, on land formerly owned by an Augustinian Priory. Much later, in April 1875, the Sandown Park Racecourse was opened on land nearby. Sandown House continued to be used as Council offices until 1992, when Elmbridge Borough Council opened a new Civic Centre off the High Street, Esher.

Postcard of Cato's Hill Bar, Esher, photographed in about 1860 from the graveyard of Christ Church. Lammas Lane runs along the edge of the graveyard: note the water pump to the right of the picture.

Rosebriars, the residence of the playwright and novelist R.C. Sherriff, in Esher Park Avenue, July 1976. This view shows the house from the kitchen garden. R.C. Sherriff, who died in 1976, became famous after the publication of his novel and play *Journey's End* in 1929, in which he related his own experiences as a young officer in the trenches in France during the First World War. He later went on to write other novels, and for many years worked in the film industry writing screenplays for Hollywood. The Rosebriars estate was purchased by Sherriff in 1931. In his will he bequeathed his estate to the local authority to be used as an arts centre. The estate was later sold for building development with the proceeds from the sale used to establish The Rosebriars Trust, which gives grants to local arts organizations.

Esher High Street, photographed in the 1890s showing The White Lion public house and row of shops. Note the two horse-drawn carts in the street.

The entrance gates to Esher Place, *c*. 1880, through which can be seen the magnificent entrance to the house itself. The history of Esher Place dates back to William I, who gave land to the Abbot of Croix St Leufroy in Normandy for use by Norman monks. In 1238 the manor became known as 'Esher Episcopi'. Bishop William Wayneflete built his manor house there in the late 1400s and this was acquired by Henry VIII in 1538, who incorporated it in his great deer-hunting park. In 1729 the estate was purchased by Henry Pelham. He demolished the Tudor house, leaving only the tower, on to which he added two new wings. In 1805 the estate was purchased by John Spicer, who knocked down the existing house leaving only the original Tudor tower as a memorial. A new house was built in the Palladian style on a knoll away from the tower to a design by Lapidge, who also designed Kingston Bridge.

Postcard of Fairholme, High Street, Esher, *c*. 1900. This was once the home of the Victorian novelist-poet George Meredith, from 1858 until 1864. Meredith went to live with Mr Francis John Williamson, the sculptor to Queen Victoria. Williamson had his studio in the house, but apparently, according to local legend, it was too noisy for him and he left to live in Copseham Cottage, before finally departing Esher for Kingston upon Thames. Fairholme was later named The Grapes and still exists today, as offices and a private house. The house was originally thought to date back to the early 1600s, but modern architectural research has shown that it is probably no earlier than the eighteenth century.

A drawing by Alan Randall of the Friends' Meeting House, Esher, in 1983, when it was used as a meeting place by The Lord Foley Lodge of the Oddfellows. Notice that the names of the trustees are written along the line of the pavement.

Inspection of flood damage in a house in Esher by staff from Esher Urban District Council in September 1968. The whole district was hit by severe flooding on 16 September of that year when the River Mole burst its banks after heavy rainfall. Other towns affected included East and West Molesey, Walton-on-Thames and Hersham.

The Embassy Cinema, Portsmouth Road, Esher, prior to it opening to the general public on 23 August 1937. The cinema was built on the site of a house owned by the Schiller brothers. It took just over a year to build the cinema and it seated 1,300 people. Today it is called the Canon, although the old name remains on the façade.

Esher post office, High Street, Esher, *c.* 1900.

'We'll nip through the agenda before 'em wakes up.' This *Surrey Comet* cartoon by Baldwin lampoons Esher Urban District Council in the 1960s. Over the years local government has come in for much criticism, especially in the 1960s when the old Esher Urban District Council was criticized in the local press for its apparent inefficiency and slothfulness. A particular concern was the failure of the authority to curb the increase in motor traffic using Esher High Street.

'Move with the Times, Indeed the Times must move with Us'; a late 1960s cartoon by Baldwin shows Esher Urban District Councillors walking along Esher High Street by a sign entitled 'Esher Welcomes Piled Up Traffic'. The figures in this cartoon are wearing labels saying 'General Shortsight', 'Outdated Ideas', 'Micawber Mentality', 'Self Interested Trader', and 'Fuddled Thinking'.

Esher Urban District Council workmen, photographed between 1895 and 1900 by F.F.J. Fricker of Esher. These men were the first paid employees of the new Esher Urban District Council which was established in 1895 and lasted until 1974, when it was replaced by Elmbridge Borough Council.

A coachman on the driver's seat photographed outside Chestnut Lodge, Esher. Mr Williamson was the coachman featured in this picture, taken in the 1880s.

A family studio portrait of Mr and Mrs Curtis with their baby son, Leslie. Leslie's father, Harold Curtis, served in the Army during the First World War.

A photograph of the VE Day celebrations in
Esher in May 1945, with two women holding
jugs. The woman in the centre of the
photograph was Kate Lampard (née Knight),
who was an aunt of Mr Leslie Curtis. The
woman on the left is a neighbour. Kate
Lampard lived above the Esher Fire Station
when it first opened in Park Road.

Mr Tom Birchmore, the Esher fishmonger,
wearing the uniform of an Air Raid Precautions
warden during the Second World War. He was
stationed at the Church of England School and
his uniform consisted of an ARP warden boiler
suit, a whistle on a chain, as well as the
regulation tin hat.

The City Arms public house in the Portsmouth Road, Esher in the 1860s. The sign 'Collard' over the doorway probably refers to the owner or licensee of the premises, because the brewery appears to be Combe and Company, judging by the sign on the right hand side of the photograph.

A Curtis family wedding photograph taken in the 1920s. The man standing in the centre is the bridegroom, Fred Lampard, who was adopted by Leslie Curtis's grandfather, who lived in Summer Road, Thames Ditton. He married Kate Knight, later Mrs Kate Lampard, who appears in a previous photograph of the Esher VE Day Celebrations in May 1945 (page 21) and is sitting in the middle of the photograph holding flowers. She is seated between her two bridesmaids. This picture was taken by the photographer W.T. Keable, of 30 Brighton Road, Surbiton.

A late nineteenth-century photograph of the last Esher beadle, James Bowler, seen here wearing his greatcoat and top hat, which was trimmed with gold lace. James Bowler was eighty years old when he died in 1930 and was employed to impound stray cattle on the village green, and to rid the area of vagrants and thieves.

A milk girl photographed next to her milk cart in front of The Bear Hotel, Esher, during the First World War. This photograph came from an album showing women's war work during the First World War, compiled between 1915 and 1918 by Arthur Reavil, a member of the Royal Photographic Society. He presented this album to Mr and Mrs S.W. Burleigh, an Esher family.

The Duchess of Albany and the Princess Alice at the inauguration of a new steamer for the Esher Fire Brigade, 1903. Princess Alice is seen standing next to the engine.

A photograph, taken in the 1880s, of a group of pupils with their schoolmaster, outside the National School for Boys, Girls and Infants, located opposite The Green, Esher. This school was built in 1858/9 by Benjamin Ferrey. After 1870 the school became subject to government inspection and financial review under the 1870 Education Act. The school was administered by the Church of England.

A studio portrait of a young woman in nurse's uniform during the First World War. This is possibly a photograph of R.C. Sherriff's sister as a VAD nurse.

Another studio portrait, this time of Cecil
H.M. Sherriff, younger brother of R.C.
Sherriff, in army uniform. Both brothers
regularly wrote to each other while on army
service during the war, and used nicknames in
their letters. R.C. Sherriff was known as 'Bon',
while C.H.M. Sherriff was 'Bundy'. C.H.M.
Sherriff was stationed in France during 1917
and 1918, and this photograph probably dates
from the last year of the First World War.

A postcard of the High Street, Esher, taken in October 1920. Notice how few people there are and no
motor cars or horses and carts.

Gardner's Butchers' shop on the corner of the High Street and Park Road, Esher, photographed in about 1900. Note the carefully arranged displays of butchered carcasses and the advertisement above the entrance door to the shop: 'By Appointment to Her Majesty the Queen and HRH The Duchess of Albany'. The butcher's delivery boy appears on the firm's delivery cart to the right of the shop premises.

Copseham Cottage, one-time home of the Victorian novelist-poet George Meredith, photographed in the 1860s. It was Meredith's home until 1864, and for many years it was the property of Sir Herbert Cook, Bart. The Hardy family lived there until 1964. The house was later demolished when the Esher bypass was built.

Workmen reducing the level of the gradient on Lammas Lane, Esher, *c.* 1910. This picture shows workmen with wooden wheelbarrows on the left of the photograph taking away the surplus soil, while labourers on the right reduce the road level by digging trenches. All the work appears to be done by pick and shovel as there are no mechanical diggers in sight. Mr Fread supervized the roadworks.

Four construction workers stand in front of some new shops being built in Esher High Street near The Bear Hotel in the 1930s. In the early 1930s, Esher High Street was redeveloped with new shopping parades replacing the earlier eighteenth- and nineteenth-century shops and houses. This building development was spurred on by the construction of new housing estates in the Hinchley Wood area, and the general increase in motor traffic brought on by the opening of the Kingston bypass in 1927. These developments in the years before the Second World War led to the transformation of Esher from a rural village into a commuter suburb of south-west London.

Mr A. Williams (1875–1965) of Esher, who
was a carpenter at The Royal Mills, Esher, and
later worked with A.C. Cars in Thames
Ditton. He is shown here as a young man
holding a wooden framer, possibly for an
aircraft wing. He is wearing his apron over his
trousers and underneath his suit, which is
typical of the everyday work clothes worn by
artisans and craftsmen during the early part of
the twentieth century.

An aerial photograph of Rosebriars, the Esher home of the playwright and novelist R.C. Sherriff, taken in
the late 1950s. It shows the house in the centre with the gardens and greenhouses at the rear.

The Queen Mother meeting one of the jockeys at the Grand Military Meeting at Sandown Park Racecourse, Esher, held in March 1959. The jockey is Mr P. Upton, who rode his horse 'Golden Drop' to victory in the Gold Cup Day race meeting.

The stands at Sandown Park Racecourse were rebuilt during the winter of 1972 to 1973. This involved the demolition of the old wooden stands and their replacement with a new state-of-the-art concrete and brick building, which provided conference and race-going facilities in the one main stand. This photograph shows the early stages of construction of the reinforced concrete framework supporting the main stand.

CLAREMONT

The lake at Claremont, photographed in the 1960s. The lake and grounds are now in the hands of the National Trust.

Claremont School, Esher, photographed in the mid-1960s. A house was built on this site by Sir John Vanburgh in 1708, the renowned playwright and architect of Blenheim Palace and Castle Howard. In about 1714 two lodges were constructed by the main gate, which still exist. A second house was built by the Earl of Clare, who later became Duke of Newcastle, and on his death in 1768, the house and gardens were sold to Lord Clive, who had recently returned to England in 1766 after his military successes in India. Lancelot Brown, the famous 'Capability' Brown, was employed to build his new house, which involved demolishing the Vanburgh house and constructing one in the fashionable Palladian style; this cost Clive over £100,000. Sadly, Clive died before the house was finished. The house had a series of private owners until it was bought by Parliament in 1816 for Prince Leopold of Saxe-Coburg and his new wife, Princess Charlotte.

Claremont, Esher.   17850

An interior view of Claremont House, photographed in the 1920s. This room has classical motifs and medallions on the walls and a large inlaid design on the marble floor. There are also classical friezes on the walls depicting scenes from antiquity. Clive of India spent a fortune on decorating the interior of Claremont. The entrance hall alone was decorated with classical scagolia (imitation stone made out of plaster mixed with glue and then coloured) and columns of the Ionic order, which cost £208 19s, while the ceiling cost £107 10s 6d and the marble flooring £192 8s. Clive also had a sunken marble bath built in the basement of the property – with a fireplace because the house was notoriously cold all year round – which cost him £310 15s 5d to complete.

Claremont, Esher.

Another view of Claremont House in the 1920s. This shows the saloon, with a mixture of furniture. Claremont became famous after 1848 because of the exiled King of France, Louis Philippe, who went to live there with his wife Queen Marie-Amelie and their courtiers. Because they were Catholics, the only place they could worship was at the tiny Roman Catholic Chapel of St Charles Borromeo in Weybridge. When the King died in 1850 he was interred in the vaults there. Queen Maria-Amelie lived at Claremont for another sixteen years until her death in 1866. Queen Victoria then owned the property and gave it to her youngest son, Leopold, Duke of Albany, who settled there with his wife Princess Helen of Waldeck in 1882. After the Duke died, in 1884, the Duchess continued to live at Claremont with their daughter Princess Alice, later Countess of Athlone, and their son, Prince Charles.

A photograph of Princess Helen and Prince Leopold, *c.* 1882.

The Duchess of Albany at Claremont with the Tecks and Saxe-Coburg-Gothas, 1907. During the First World War the house became a convalescent home for officers, and later a military hospital run by Mr and Mrs Paget. After the war the Duchess let Claremont to a girl's school, while she lived at Loseberry in Claygate. The Duchess of Albany died in 1922 in Innsbruck while on holiday. Claremont did not revert to her son, the Duke of Saxe-Coburg and Gotha, as he was a German citizen and had fought in the German army during the First World War. The property was confiscated by the Government who sold it to Sir William Corry, director of the Cunard Steamship Company.

Mr Alfred Burr, coachman to the Duchess of Albany, holding his baby son Richard while in the stable yard at Claremont, *c.* 1912. In later life Richard Burr became a well-known and respected Esher historian.

A horse and trap in the stable yard at Claremont, *c.* 1912. The property had a succession of private owners after the First World War until it was purchased by the Christian Scientists for use as a school. During the Second World War it was used to house drawing-office staff moved from the Hawkers Aircraft Company, based at Kingston upon Thames.

WEST END, ESHER

A group of school children standing outside the Infants' School, which was opposite the common, West End, Esher, photographed before the First World War.

A group of boys photographed just before playing a cricket match at West End, Esher in 1929. The boys, who all came from Portsmouth Road and Station Road as well as from the Ditton Marsh area, organized the match themselves.

A very rustic view of the Albany Bridge over the River Mole, looking from Hersham towards Esher, c. 1900. The bridge was called Albany Bridge in honour of the Duke and Duchess of Albany who lived nearby at Claremont, in the nineteenth century.

A photograph of The Prince of Wales public house in West End, Esher, *c.* 1963, taken from the corner of the common. The buildings behind the public house were once used by Watney & Co. to brew beer. There had been a brewery there since 1841, Watney's took over in 1899. Brewing ceased during the First World War. Thereafter the premises were used by a coal merchant. Now they are an annexe of the pub. Mr Frank Plowman had a boot and saddlery repair shop in the former brewery.

A photograph of Penny Lansdell aged four, and Mick Barrow aged sixty-four, at West End Pond, Esher, in 1963. Mr Barrow is sailing a toy boat on the pond. People have gathered around the West End Pond for recreational purposes, such as sailing toy boats, for many years.

A family sitting on the grass outside The Chequers public house, on West End Common, Esher, *c.* 1900. The Chequers was a low L-shaped building and was an inn until about 1918. It dates from the seventeenth or eighteenth century and was a notorious smuggler's retreat; according to local folklore, Jerry Abershaw and Dick Turpin took refuge there. It once had a skittle alley and a blacksmith's premises attached to the inn.

This is a view of West End, Esher, taken from a postcard published by Fricker of Esher in about 1906. The children are playing beside the flooded pool. The Prince of Wales public house can be seen in the background and beyond that the brewery, which operated until the First World War.

A postcard, *c.* 1910, of a group of children sitting beside West End Pond, Esher, with The Chequers in the background. These children are thought to come from the public house.

Jubilee Cottages, West End, Esher, built at the time of Queen Victoria's Diamond Jubilee in 1897.

A photograph, taken in 1894, of the floods which affected the Hersham Road near Albany Bridge, West End, Esher.

Talbot Lodge, West End, Esher, photographed on 7 December 1978. Formerly called Glenhurst, Talbot Lodge was once the home of Colonel and Lady Emma Talbot. Emma was the daughter of Lord Derby and had been bridesmaid to Queen Victoria's eldest daughter. The Colonel, the Hon. Sir W.P. Talbot was Sergeant-at-Arms of the House of Lords for forty years and was very well liked in the Esher area. Talbot Lodge has since been demolished.

EAST MOLESEY

A postcard of a river barge and tugboat at Molesey Lock, photographed in the 1950s. Before the coming of the railway, the River Thames was the main artery for transporting large quantities of freight traffic by horse-drawn or sailing barge. In times of drought certain parts of the river became too shallow to allow the barges to pass, particularly the bend near Molesey Hurst, known locally as 'Hampton Shoals'. A local engineer, John Rennie, proposed that several weirs be built to hold back the water, with special pound locks to let the barges through. Work began on a pound lock at Molesey in 1814, and it was opened in August 1815; it was 168 feet long and 30 feet wide with a fall of 6 feet. The lock keepers were paid 32 shillings a week, until 1852 when their wages were cut to 18 shillings due to the decline in river traffic caused by the fierce competition from the railway companies. In 1871 roller slides were added to the main basin, to allow the easy passage of rowing boats, skiffs, and other pleasure craft which were beginning to use the river. It was now possible to travel from one level to another without having to use the lock at all. The lock has been rebuilt twice, first in 1906, and again in 1959 when it was completely restored and modernized, with electric controls to operate the gates.

A postcard of the Weir, Molesey, postmarked 27 February 1907. It shows a man fishing from the Weir, which has been a famous Molesey landmark for many years. The French Impressionist artist, Alfred Sisley, stayed in the Molesey area in 1874 painting many river scenes, including one of Molesey Weir.

A view of a packed Molesey lock, photographed in the early 1900s. This postcard view clearly demonstrates the huge numbers of people who came down to the River Thames every summer for pleasure boating in the years before 1914.

Another early twentieth-century postcard, this time of 'Tagg's Island, Hampton Court', posted on 9 August 1904. It shows four women in a boat in mid-river, with skiffs moored in the foreground. The Tagg family have had a long association with the River Thames, since the 1830s when John Tagg hired out boats and fishing tackle. One of his sons, Thomas George Tagg, reconstructed a boathouse on Walnut Tree Island, later called Platt's Ait (finally known as Tagg's Island) in 1868. Then he started a boatbuilding business, and, by the 1870s, was constructing launches which were shown at international exhibitions in Britain and France. Soon he leased the whole island including the public house, The Angler's Retreat. In a short time the whole island had been transformed from a backwater into a pleasure resort, with a hotel and leisure facilities. These facilities attracted British and European royalty, and the aristocracy, who mingled with more common folk. In 1889 Thomas Tagg branched out into another business venture, and constructed a large, ornate and luxurious clubhouse on three acres of land facing Walnut Tree Island on the Molesey shore. It contained a ballroom, a reading room, a private dining room, a members lavatory and a ladies drawing room. Other features included a secretary's room, a bar, and six large bedrooms on the second floor and a bathroom and lavatory with hot and cold water. The premises also had electric light, telephones and electric bells. It was opened on 2 May 1891. Unfortunately Thomas Tagg did not live long to see it flourish as he died in 1897 after catching a cold; his son George John Tagg took over the business. However, by the time of the Boer War, high society had moved on to other locations and Tagg's went into liquidation. The assets were sold off in 1904 although the clubhouse survived in use as small factory units. Tagg's continued to run the hotel on Tagg's Island, which later became the famous Fred Karno's Karsino, a luxurious hotel and ballroom which was constructed on the island to replace the existing hotel and public house. The new building was opened on Sunday 22 June 1913 at a cost of over £40,000. This rather odd-looking wooden building survived until 1971, when it was demolished. At the time it was described by *The Times* as 'one of the strangest buildings in Britain'.

Walton Road, East Molesey, photographed in the 1920s. The road was created in the 1860s when Molesey was gradually developed into a suburb of south-west London and new shops and houses were built on land between Molesey Lock and Hampton Court. This new building created a population explosion in the area, which grew from 765 people in 1851 to 2,409 by 1871. Large mansions had existed in the area before the development of Walton Road. A prominent building was called The Lodge, formerly Moulsey Villa, and was situated just south of Ivy Lodge in the present day Molesey Road. The house was owned in the 1780s by Jenkin Jones, a wealthy distiller. Later on in the nineteenth century, Sir Stephen Shairp, British ambassador to Russia, lived there. The house served as a seminary for young ladies until it was bought by Dr John Cockle, the noted Victorian physician. It survived until 1973 when it was demolished to make way for the Dene housing estate. Another large mansion was called The Grove and was the family home of some notable families such as the Palmers and the Hothams; during the 1820s it was owned by the Rt Hon John Wilson Croker, a noted politician who is reputed to have suggested the name Conservative for the Tory party. Its first private owners were the Barrow family; in 1932 it was bought by Faraday House Electrical College as a sports club. After 1945 it was owned by Bentalls, the Kingston upon Thames department store and was later sold to Elmbridge Borough Council for housing purposes. However, before it could be preserved, the house was destroyed by fire in May 1975 and later demolished.

A postcard of the Cow Common, East Molesey, *c.* 1920.

A postcard of The Bell public house, East Molesey, issued in 1969.

Floods in Walton Road, East Molesey, 1928. This view shows two men in a rowing boat in the foreground and a horse and trap in the middle distance. The Molesey area has been prey to flooding for many years; the last floods to occur in the area happened in September 1968 when the River Mole burst its banks and flooded many towns in the district, including Hersham and Walton-on-Thames.

An old petrol pump run by Patching and Sons, photographed in front of their shop premises in Walton Road, East Molesey, in October 1974.

The Molesey Boat Club house, seen from the towpath, in October 1974. The sign reads, 'Danger River in Flood. Turn at Cricket Pavilion. Keep Club Side of Island'.

Walton Road, East Molesey, in 1977.

A photograph of a footpath leading to East Molesey Common, taken in the 1960s. On the right is a small cottage and a boundary wall; the footpath is blocked to vehicles by the cement posts.

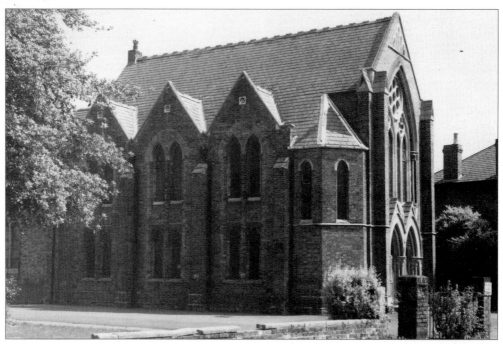

East Molesey Methodist Church, Manor Road, East Molesey, in 1977. Methodists first held services in the Molesey area in the 1840s and, by 1867, had built a church hall in Manor Road, which also doubled as a Sunday school. In 1877 a new church building was opened providing accommodation for 350 people. A new Sunday school was built in 1885 which provided fourteen classrooms and a main hall.

The Old Manor House in East Molesey, *c.* 1960. This building dated from the late 1500s, although it was much altered over the years. It was known as The Limes for much of its life until it was called The Old Manor House in the 1930s. It was demolished in 1963 and replaced by an old people's home built by Esher Urban District Council. The name Molesey is derived from the Saxon word for an island, 'Egl', linked to the name of the owner, 'Mul'. So Molesey meant 'Mule's Island' or 'meadow land'. Over the years the name has been spelt Mulesey, Molesey, or in the nineteenth century as Moulsey, until Molesey was adopted as the recognized version. The Domesday Survey of 1086 recorded three manors tenanted by knights who had settled in the area from Normandy. Henry VIII incorporated Molesey into his royal hunting estate, 'The Honor of Hampton Court'. However, it was the coming of the railway to East Molesey in February 1849 that led to the development of the area from a rural backwater into a commuter town. It was not until 1895 that the area gained its own local government when Parliament created separate Urban District Councils for East and West Molesey. They were later combined with Esher Urban District Council in 1933, which in turn became part of Elmbridge Borough Council in 1974.

Esher Road, East Molesey, in December 1971.

Another view of Esher Road, East Molesey, in December of the same year.

Mr J.G. Armes with his two sons, standing outside his shop in Molesey, *c.* 1915. The shop sold fittings for electric and gas lights, as well as offering general electrical engineering and fitting.

A fine print of St Mary the Virgin, the Parish Church for East Molesey, by Samuel Woodburn, *c.* 1807. It was published by Evans in 1819. There was a small church there made out of wood from at least the twelfth century. The medieval church, which was described in 1760 as a 'pretty little rustic structure', was soon too small to accommodate the expanding population of the area, as it could only seat 135 people. On 7 December 1863 the church caught fire and, although it was quickly extinguished, it did mean the parochial authorities had to commission a replacement church. A new church was then built and consecrated on 17 October 1865. A tower with a spire and a north aisle were added in 1867 and a south aisle in 1883. The last addition was an extension to the chancel in 1926–7.

A mobile coal office in the goods yard at Hampton Court Station in 1963 or 1964. The words on the back door of the van are 'Tyne Main Coal Company'. Views like this are a thing of the past because there are now no goods yards attached to suburban railway stations in the immediate area; most were closed in the 1960s and 1970s and the goods traffic went by road. Domestic coal consumption has dropped dramatically as most homes are now fitted with gas-fired central heating. The mobile coal office was situated at Hampton Court station during works at Tolworth Coal Concentration Depot. It was well appointed with two desks and a telephone.

Three shops in Walton Road, East Molesey in August 1963. The shops are the Electricity Shop on the left, B. Stroud, a decorating shop in the centre, and a fish and chip shop on the right.

The forecourt of K.C.S. Garage in Walton Road, East Molesey, in August 1963.

A postcard view of St Paul's Church, East Molesey, dated 9 April 1904. This was opened in 1856 to serve a new housing estate. The tower and spire were added in 1888.

Bridge Road, East Molesey, c. 1908–9. This view looks across to the Carnarvon Hotel on the left and Tagg's Hotel on the right. In the street, which is covered with gravel and some horse manure, can be seen a few pedestrians, two horse-drawn carts and a man on a bicycle.

Moore's Estate Agents premises at 1 Creek Road, East Molesey, in the 1960s. This photograph shows Mr Harry Moore with his son Victor. Moore & Sons had had premises in Creek Road since 1867; prior to that the family ran a painting and decorating business. Creek Road or Lane was a narrow road that ran from the Ferry between some old houses on its north side and past the willow-lined Creek or Mole, due south on to the site of the present police station. Further on it ran round a sharp bend which was known as The Corner and later as Elphick's Corner, after Mr Elphick who owned a butcher's shop and slaughter house nearby.

No. 1 Creek Road, East Molesey as a private house, before it became Moore's business premises. This photograph was taken in the 1860s..

Inspection of the Molesey Fire Brigade at Hampton on 25 May 1902. This was after they had won the 'All Surrey' turnout for speed and appearance. The firemen in this photograph are Mr A. Lincoln, engineer; Mr W. Spicer, driver; Mr C. Carpenter and Mr F. Colley, both firemen. The inspection was made by Sir E. Massey Shaw, KCB, the Duchess of Marlborough and Colonel Dixon.

Radnor House, an eighteenth-century mansion in Walton Road, East Molesey, shortly before it was demolished and replaced by the present modern building of the same name.

HRH the Queen and the Queen Mother attending a race meeting at Hurst Park Racecourse in the 1950s. Horse racing had taken place at the Hurst since at least 1737 and by the 1860s it had become an organized annual event, with an autumn race season too. The races were known as 'The Cockney Derby' for many years on account of people travelling from London to attend them. Charles Dickens wrote a description of the races at the Hurst in *Nicholas Nickelby*. In 1890 the racecourse re-opened as Hurst Park Racecourse after a three-year refurbishment which provided new stands and fencing around the course. The racecourse survived until October 1962 after which it was sold off for redevelopment. Many of the fittings were auctioned off including the largest grandstand which was sold to Mansfield Town Football Club and was transported in six huge sections. A housing estate now occupies most of the site of the old racecourse.

Two jockeys jumping a fence at Hurst Park Racecourse in the 1950s.

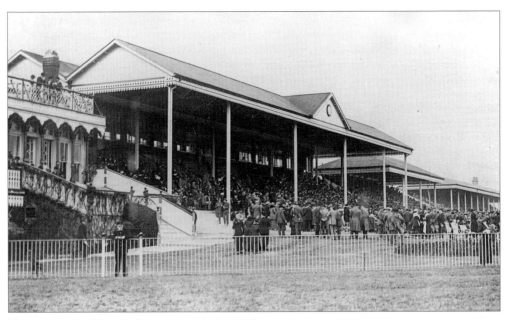

The grandstand at Hurst Park Racecourse in the 1950s.

East Molesey Fire Brigade outside their original fire station, photographed in 1897, the year of Queen Victoria's Diamond Jubilee. A volunteer fire brigade was formed in 1872 and the equipment was purchased from Messrs Merryweather, the famous fire equipment manufacturers. Two years later, in 1874, the fire brigade rented accommodation in Park Road to house the equipment which consisted of hoses, standpipes, a lamp and a handcart. In 1899 a steam fire pump was purchased to replace the manually-operated pump and the fire brigade moved to new premises on the corner of Matham and Walton Roads, provided by the East Molesey Local Board. The new steam pump was horse-drawn, and uniforms and other equipment were purchased. Molesey Urban District Council was established in 1895 and took over responsibility for running the service. It erected a new purpose-built fire station in Walton Road, East Molesey, which was opened on 5 October 1902. In 1925 a petrol-driven fire engine made by Dennis in Guildford was purchased for £800. It had a 35 foot long escape ladder and was a great improvement on what had been used before. In 1947 all the local fire brigades were amalgamated under the control of Surrey County Council, and Molesey fire station was closed in 1961.

The Osborne family, photographed in 1918 when the family lived in Surbiton. Ella Osborne is on the left wearing glasses, next to her is her little sister in the pushchair, while her two brothers are standing either side of her mother. The Osborne family later went to live in East Molesey.

The remains of Hurst Park Racecourse stand after it was burnt down in June 1913. The fire was started by the suffragette Kitty Marion.

Smelt's horse-drawn pantechnican removal van photographed at their yard in Esher, *c.* 1914. Smelt's were based in the Esher, Molesey and Thames Ditton areas.

Mrs Smelt, wife of Mr Smelt, owner of the removal business, with her four children, sitting on the veranda of a horse-drawn caravan with a friend, *c.* 1914.

A caravan on a plot of land known as Mimosas, East Molesey. The caravan appears to have originally been an old railway carriage, which is propped up beside a tree, and may possibly date from the 1850s.

WEST MOLESEY

A pen and ink drawing by R. Burton of The Royal Oak public house in West Molesey, in the 1970s, with the tower of St Peter's Parish Church in the background. There is a reference in the Domesday Survey of 1086 to the existence of a church in West Molesey. It says that: 'Odard hold Molesham, which was held by King Edward by Tovi. It was then rated at 6 hides and 1 virgate, now at 1 hide. There are 2 carucates of arable land : one is in demesne, and there are ten villains and five cottars with 4 carucates. There is a Church, and two bondmen. In the time of King Edward it was valued at 100 shillings; afterwards 50 shillings; now at 4 pounds.' The present building dates from the thirteenth century and consists of an embattled western tower of flint and rubble with pinnacles as well as a clock and two bells. The chancel consists of stone enclosing some early brasses, one of which bears an inscription to 'Thomas Brende esq, of West Molesey, ob. 1598.'

The Canon public house in the High Street, West Molesey, 1963.

Rose Cottages in Molesey Road, West Molesey, in the 1960s. They have since been demolished.

Children from St Barnabas' School, West Molesey, with the museum they set up in their own classroom in 1973. Some of these items have now been donated to Elmbridge Museum.

An eighteenth-century painting of West Molesey parish church.

A view of Walton Road, West Molesey, *c.* 1971, showing the parish church in the background and an advertisement hoarding on a building in the foreground.

An engraved portrait of Admiral, the Hon. Sir George Cranfield Berkeley who is buried in a vault beneath West Molesey parish church. A monument in the church reads: 'In a vault beneath this spot lie the remains of the Honourable George Cranfield Berkeley, second son of Augustus, fourth Earl of Berkeley – Knight Grand Cross of the most honourable order of the Bath, and Lord High Admiral of Portugal during the successful struggle of that nation against the French usurpation – like many of his ancestors he devoted his life to the sea service of his country – he died the 24th of February 1818, aged sixty-four years and six months.'

HINCHLEY WOOD

The Park, Hinchley Wood, in 1984. Hinchley Wood was built in the 1930s on land acquired from local farmers by speculative property developers, most of the land being purchased from Couchmore Farm. The largest estate was built by Messrs E.& L. Berg. The opening of the Kingston bypass in 1927 and Hinchley Wood railway station by the Southern Railway in 1930, helped bring new homeowners into the immediate area bordering Esher village. Housing development continued up until the outbreak of the Second World War. The Hinchley Wood Residents Association was established in 1932 to 'make Hinchley Wood a better place to live in'.

No. 53 Greenways, Hinchley Wood, destroyed by a V1 flying bomb in 1944.

Hinchley Wood Hotel, Manor Road North, in 1962.

The Hinchley Wood Hotel sign, Manor Road
North, in 1962.

A lorry on the Kingston bypass in 1962. Notice the absence of traffic.

Old fashioned road signs at a road junction in Hinchley Wood, in 1962. Note the kerb stones which are painted black and white.

Open countryside near Hinchley Wood, photographed in the 1950s.

Manor Farm in Claygate Lane, Hinchley Wood, 1952. Suburbia existed side-by-side with local farms and open countryside.

End of a country lane

Now bordered by schools and a church where formerly there were only fields alongside i pot holed and often muddy surface, Claygate Lane, Hinchley Wood, is fast being turned into modern road with footpaths on each side.

A newspaper article from the late 1930s showing the development of Claygate Lane, Hinchley Wood.

VE Day celebrations in Greenways, Hinchley Wood, May 1945. Impromptu street parties were held throughout the country in May and June 1945 to celebrate Victory in Europe, and were organized by local residents. Most young men were still in the forces at this time, and street parties, like the one pictured here, were attended mainly by women and children. The Second World War did not finish until Japan surrendered in August 1945, so official Victory celebrations were not held in London until June 1946.

THAMES DITTON

Ye Olde Swan Hotel, Thames Ditton, depicted on a postcard issued in the 1960s.

An earlier view of Ye Olde Swan Hotel, Thames Ditton, in 1908.

Thames Ditton, from the river, April 1908.

A postcard of a house built on the Pound Farm Estate, Thames Ditton, by Buckley Builders of Ember Lane, Esher, in 1922 to 1923. They built four types of houses; this was type A1.

House type A4 built by Buckley Builders on the Pound Farm Estate, Thames Ditton, in 1922 to 1923.

St Nicholas Church, Thames Ditton, in the 1950s. First mention of a church at Thames Ditton is in the years between 1115 and 1125 when King Henry I allowed Gilbert, the High Sherriff of Surrey who had founded Merton Abbey, to grant four chapelries to Kingston, one of which was Thames Ditton. In the 1300s the church was enlarged with the addition of the 'Chapel of our Lady' on the north side of the chancel, and one hundred years later a north aisle was added. In 1639 Sir Dudley Carleton of Imber Court planned to build a new chapel to the south side of the church but this work was never carried out. It was not until 1676 that a second chapel was built on the north side as a burial chapel for the Hatton family. By 1781 the chapel had to be restored because it had fallen into disrepair. In 1837 a new north aisle was completed. A proposal, which was never fulfilled, was made to erect a new church seating 700 people. In 1864 a new south aisle was completed, and since then the church has received no further alterations. The font is reputed to be Norman and the church brasses date from the latter half of the sixteenth century.

Rectory Lane, Ditton Hill, *c.* 1900.

Southville Road, Thames Ditton, in 1934.

The interior of the Thames Ditton Bronze Foundry, 1907. The equestrian statue in the background is of the Duke of Cambridge sculpted by Adrian Hones. On the shelf to the right are plaster patterns for the Hyde Park statue 'Physical Energy' by G.F. Watts. The Thames Ditton Bronze Foundry was established in 1874 by Cox and Sons, who turned out statues of leading worthies, such as Captain James Cook, The Duke of Wellington and General Gordon of Khartoum. In 1897 Messrs Hollinshead and Burton took over. Queen Victoria was a popular subject, others included 'Physical Energy' by the sculptor G.F. Watts, and 'Persimmion' by Adrian Jones of the horse that won the 1896 Derby for the Prince of Wales – later King Edward VII. Perhaps the greatest achievement of the foundry was the 'Peace Quadriga' by Adrian Jones, which was erected on Hyde Park Corner in 1912. The foundry closed in 1939.

Mr E.J. Chaser, carrying out some finishing work on the statue of Mrs Pankhurst by A.G. Walker, in 1930.

A photograph showing the exterior of the
Thames Ditton Bronze Foundry, in the 1930s.

A studio portrait of Mr F. W. Braddock,
sandmoulder and chief assistant at the Thames
Ditton Bronze Foundry, c. 1890 to 1900. The
longest serving manager of the works was Mr
Arthur Brian Burton who worked from 1900
until 1933.

Renwick Steam Car, loaded with life-size bronze figures of soldiers for use in part of a war memorial in the 1920s. The foundry was particularly busy casting figures for war memorials up and down the country after the First World War.

Cyclists outside the Angel Hotel, Thames Ditton, 1896. This was a favourite meeting place for cyclists at the end of the nineteenth century. They rode down the Portsmouth Road through Esher and then onto Ripley; the Portsmouth Road was known by them as the Ripley Road.

A dramatic photograph showing the collapse, due to subsidence, of shops at Winters Bridge, Thames Ditton, in 1908. Notice the policeman guarding the shops.

Mr R. Attwell BEM, scoutmaster of the Thames Ditton Troop for thirty-nine years, is seen here saluting a young cub. Attwell died in 1948 aged eighty and was known as 'Silver Wolf' by his troop. He lived at 21 Angel Road, Thames Ditton.

Pedestrians in Ferry Road, Winters Bridge, Thames Ditton, *c.* 1910.

King Haaker of Norway visiting a war factory in Thames Ditton in 1944. With him are the Crown Prince (later King Olav I) and Lord Mountevans who was known affectionately as Evans of the 'Broke'.

A brass of Erasmus and Schwyn Forde in St Nicholas Church, Thames Ditton, dating from the 1550s.

Thames Ditton High Street, *c.* 1900.

Post Office Corner, Thames Ditton High Street, photographed under snow, during the winter of 1916 to 1917.

The Home of Compassion of Jesus, formerly Boyle Farm, Thames Ditton, *c.* 1920. Once known as Boyle Farm House, this building dates from the eighteenth century and was bought in 1903 by the Reverend Mother of the Community of the Compassion of Jesus – a Church of England religious community. The house has a chapel which is under the care of the vicar of West Molesey.

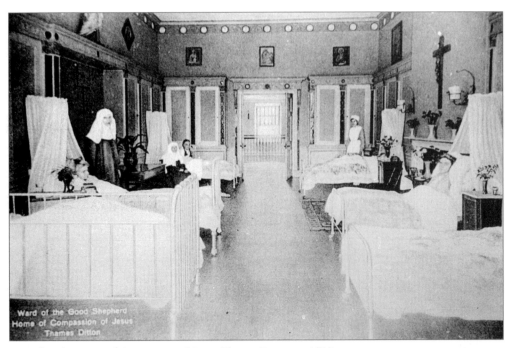

A ward in the Home of Compassion of Jesus, Thames Ditton, *c.* 1920.

Surrey Fire Brigade attended a fire at A.C. Cars Works in Thames Ditton, on the night of 27 and 28 February 1958. This photograph shows the fire tender outside the charred premises on the following morning.

Mr and Mrs S. Mercer of Thames Ditton practising
archery in their garden, c. 1910.

The Revd R. Wild, blessing the restored weather
vane of St Nicholas Church, in July 1952. The
curate, the Revd Gilbert Cheetham, is standing
behind him.

Miss M. Chisman in the doorway of her house,
Fowler Cottage, Thames Ditton, *c.* 1890.

A view from the roof of The Swan Inn (Hotel) of The Crown Inn and Batchelors Hall, Thames Ditton,
photographed on a summer's day before 1925. A large advert for Isleworth Ales is painted on the
weatherboarding on the side of The Crown Inn.

The bar of the old Crown Inn before it was demolished in 1925 and replaced with a modern building.

Mrs J. Henderson, a Thames Ditton resident, standing on a platform at Surbiton railway station in the 1920s.

Members of the Thames Ditton Skiff Club
parading through Thames Ditton at the head of
a wedding procession for the Fenton family,
c. 1924. They are walking in front of the
wedding car carrying their rowing oars.

A car photographed outside High House, Thames Ditton, in the 1930s. High House was later demolished
and replaced by the premises of A.C. Cars.

Members of the Henderson family riding a motorcycle in the Thames Ditton area, *c.* 1924. This photograph is taken from a Henderson family album.

The Fountain in Thames Ditton, *c.* 1900.

LONG DITTON

The foot of Ditton Hill, Long Ditton, showing two Edwardian ladies in a horse and trap, c. 1910. Ditton Hill Road runs from the junction with Fleece Road, near the London to Southampton railway line, into Ditton Road which eventually joins up with the Ewell Road and Surbiton. Today the area is built over with modern housing but when this photograph was taken at the turn of the century, it was still a very rural area, miles away from the urban sprawl of south-west London.

Children performing in a school play at St Mary's School, Long Ditton, *c.* 1919.

A class of girls at St Mary's School, Long Ditton, in 1919.

The Mason's Arms public house, Long Ditton during the great floods of 1894. The Mason's Arms was owned by Hodgson's Brewery who were based in Kingston upon Thames.

The Mason's Arms public house, Long Ditton, photographed after 1886.

A watercolour of The New Inn public house, Long Ditton, *c.* 1865. The steam train in the background is travelling on the London Waterloo to Southampton main line which opened in 1838.

Long Ditton School football team, 1928–9.

A contemporary print of the opening of the Lambeth Water Company's works at Long Ditton on 30 April 1852. The Lambeth Waterworks Company supplied water to London from its works along the River Thames. The works were built to supply water to the new town of New Kingston – later called Kingston-on-Railway, and finally known as Surbiton – as well as Kingston upon Thames, Long Ditton and Thames Ditton, Esher, and the Molesey area. London's private water companies were merged into the Metropolitan Water Board by The Metropolis Water Act of 1902. The original water basins at Seething Wells, near Thames Ditton, are now used as filter beds.

A lone cyclist walking his bicyle up Ditton Hill in 1905.

The interior of St Mary's Church, Long Ditton, c. 1900. This building dates from 1878 to 1880 and is built of Godalming stone in the architectural style of the thirteenth century. It was designed by George Edmund Street and contained some good stained glass. It was built to replace an earlier brick-built Georgian church, although there has been a church in the area since the twelfth century.

The Church Lad's Brigade, Long Ditton, *c.* 1910.

Giles' shop next door to The Globe public house in Brighton Road, on the edge of Long Ditton and Surbiton, pre-1870.

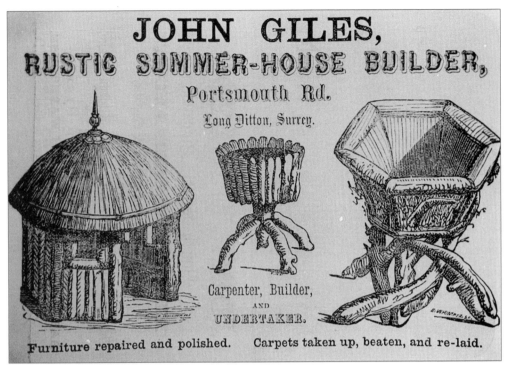

Giles' trade card advertising rustic furniture and building services, Long Ditton, *c.* 1870.

Buttery's and Hammerton's Boat building yard in Ferry Road, Long Ditton, *c.* 1900.

WESTON GREEN, ESHER

A postcard view of Weston Green, Esher, posted on 21 October 1919 showing the green in the foreground with houses on the right. It was sent to Mrs R. Smart in Wolverhampton from W. Randall, Weston Road, Weston Green, Esher.

The Pond, Weston Green, Esher, *c.* 1930.

A group of cyclists and their friends in the garden of Ye Olde Harrow Inn, Weston Green, *c.* 1900.

A large group of men standing outside Dunstone's shop in Weston Green, Esher, *c.* 1901. George Dunstone established a building business in Weston Green in the 1860s. He married Louisa Harriet Kent in Brighton in 1854 and was a staunch family man and a churchwarden at All Saint's Church, Weston Green. By 1899 the business had flourished and he employed about twenty people.

A portrait of George Dunstone in uniform as the fire brigade engineer for the Ditton and Claygate Fire Brigade, of which he was a founder member in the 1890s. George Dunstone was born in 1835 and died in 1905 aged nearly seventy years.

The funeral procession for George Dunstone passing the family shop, Weston Green, Esher, 1905. The hearse is being pulled by firemen from the local brigades. He was buried in Thames Ditton churchyard.

Little Bradley, formerly Laurel Cottage on the left and Blandford Cottage in the centre in Weston Green Road, Weston Green, Esher, photographed in about 1950.

Mr and Mrs H.M. Whale, former residents of Laurel Cottage, Weston Green Road, Long Ditton, *c.* 1910.

Marney's Pond with the Old Red House in the background, *c.* 1918.

All Saints Church, with Marney's Pond in the foreground, *c.* 1939. The foundation stone was laid in 1938 and the church was consecrated in 1939.

Roasting a sheep on Weston Green in 1893.

The Cricketers public house, owned by the Courage Brewery, Weston Green, Esher, photographed in April 1987. Notice the skip in the front of the building.

The war memorial in the Garden of Remembrance, All Saints Church, Weston Green, Esher. This photograph was taken after a wreath laying ceremony on Remembrance Sunday, 11 November 1986.

Houses facing the green, Weston Green, Esher, photographed in April 1987.

The façade of The Greyhound public house, Weston Green, April 1987.

Ye Olde Harrow Inn, Weston Green, Esher, photographed in about 1900.

Weston Green showing The Cricketers public house, *c.* 1900. At the time it was owned by Hodgson's Kingston upon Thames brewery. This card was produced by Frickers, series number 45.

Another view of Ye Olde Harrow Inn, this time in the early 1930s, showing a Mann, Crossman and Paulin brewers delivery van parked in the forecourt of the public house. By this date the inn had been totally rebuilt.

A print of Weston Green chapel, Gothic cottage and school in the nineteenth century. The Weston Green Congregational church now occupies this site in Speer Road.

CLAYGATE

The shopping parade in Claygate in the 1960s.

A traffic jam outside The Swan Inn on the Green, Claygate in the late 1950s. A cricket match is being played on the Green in the background.

A parade in Claygate in 1937 to celebrate the coronation of King George VI. This view shows two men wheeling a decorated bicycle in front of the camera.

A coloured postcard of Claygate High Street produced by the Francis Frith Company, showing the junction where the High Street meets Church Road, St Leonards Road, and Hare Lane. The post office is on the extreme left, out of view of the camera. This view was probably photographed in the 1960s.

A colour postcard view of The Red Cross Depot, Claygate, photographed during the First World War.

Leveret Cricket Club members standing in front of the rebuilt Swan Inn just after the First World War. The Swan Inn dates back to 1716 and comprised an alehouse, courtyard, garden and orchard. It was purchased by the Isleworth Brewery in 1887 and subsequently rebuilt in 1906. Leveret Cricket Club, originally Hare Lane Cricket Club, played matches in Claygate from the early 1900s on a pitch beside the Hare and Hounds public house. However, the landlord of The Swan Inn offered better amenities and the club then transferred itself to a new ground near Hare Lane Green. The legend over the sign doorway reads, 'Isleworth Brewery Ales Stouts Wines and Spirits'.

A photograph of Mr William Martin, postmaster and newsagent, pictured with his dog in Oaken Lane, Claygate, *c.* 1910.

A London and South Western railway train pulling into Claygate station, *c.* 1910. The LSWR opened a new railway line from London via Claygate to Guildford in 1885. Services were all steam hauled until the route was electrified by the Southern Railway in 1925.

Ruxley Towers, Claygate, at the time of the coronation of Queen Elizabeth II, 1953. Ruxley Lodge was the seat of Lord Foley from 1870, after it was purchased by Henry Thomas, the fifth Baron. The Ruxley estate of 100 acres, which included a large house, farmhouse and a cottage, was purchased for £22,500. At that time the house was a simple brick building which was later substantially altered and developed with the addition of towers, a swimming pool, a west wing and a conservatory. Henry died in 1905 leaving the estate to his brother, Fitzalan Charles John, who became the sixth Baron. In 1919 the seventh Baron sold the contents of the house and thereafter leased the property to private owners. During the Second World War the NAAFI used it as their headquarters, building a Nissan hut complex in the grounds. The General and Municipal Workers Union (GMWU) purchased the estate from them in 1961, turning the house into offices. In 1994, the Union sold part of the house to Bryant Homes Southern, of Binfield near Bracknell, who converted the main part of the original house into town houses. The rest of the site remains in the ownership of the General and Municipal Workers Union.

Edwardian ladies photographed at Claygate Flower Show, c. 1903. The first Claygate and District Flower Show was held on the former cricket ground on Claygate Common on 22 July 1903 and remained there until it was moved in the 1940s to the Claygate Recreation Ground. Apart from showing flowers and vegetables the show has grown into a social event, with musical performances, a dog show, exhibitions, children's activities and a huge funfair, as well as stalls belonging to local traders. In 1982 over 7,000 tickets were sold.

The Parade, Claygate, looking eastwards from the railway station, *c.* 1910. These shops were all constructed in 1897 – North and Co., House Agents, have their premises on the left of the picture.

A postcard of the Council schools, Claygate, *c.* 1910. This school was built by the Thames Ditton and Claygate School Board on land in Elm Road and opened in 1886. The first headmaster was Mr George Pack and the school had forty-nine infant pupils. The school catered for boys and girls as well. The building was hit by a bomb on 9 November 1940, forcing the school to close for three months.

Claygate Police Constable Fawsey outside The Hare and Hounds public house, Claygate, in the 1930s.

Swedenborgian Church, off Hare Lane, Claygate, photographed in about 1909. This was the New Jerusalem Church, known as the Swedenborgian Church, and was built in 1909 at the cost of £800 by Charles Higby, a local builder. Services were held in the building until the 1940s. During the Second World War it was used as an ARP Wardens' shelter. In 1951 the building was purchased by the Christian Scientists who replaced it with a new building in 1961.

Holy Trinity Church, Claygate, *c.* 1930. The Church of The Holy Trinity was built in 1840 at a cost of £1,350 which included a sum of £50 for the purchase of the land. The money was raised by subscription from seven subscribers, one of whom was Leopold, King of the Belgians, who had been living at Claremont house from 1816. A school was built adjacent to the church in 1838 and was enlarged in 1849 and again in 1866. The church was designed by Mr H. Kendal, and was originally built with one tower; it received a second one in 1866. The building was enlarged in 1866 with the addition of a new chancel and transepts at a cost of £2,000.

The footpath to Claygate Golf Links, *c.* 1910.

The footpath to Arbrook Common, Claygate, *c.* 1910.

The shopping parade, Claygate, *c.* 1930.

James Wellbelove and colleagues from Claygate brickworks striking up a merry tune in 1898. One man is playing the violin, while two are playing banjos and the fourth is on the accordian. The Wellbelove family had a long association with brickmaking in the Claygate area. Jack Wellbelove started work in the family-owned Common Road brickyard in 1888 aged twelve years old, working alongside his father, nine brothers and a nephew. Jack finally retired from brickmaking in 1964 aged eighty-eight.

Workers from the Oaken Lane brickyard, Claygate, in the early 1900s. Sims and Sons owned two brickyards in the Oaken Lane area of Claygate, and by 1911 they were producing 3 million bricks and tiles a year. However, this thriving industry located on the edge of Claygate village caused health problems. Malcom Peebles writing in *The Claygate Book* states that: 'In 1900, the council's (Esher Urban District Council) Medical Officer for Health reported that household refuse used for brickmaking caused a recurring nuisance at Claygate Station where it was unloaded – "especially in mild weather, when it undergoes putrefaction, accompanied by the emission of a horrible stench" '.

Crowds at the Claygate Flower Show in the 1940s.

Claygate Brass Band, *c.* 1900.

Claygate brickworkers and their dogs photographed outside The Winning Horse public house, *c.* 1913. This pub was built in about 1897 on waste land in Coverts Road, Claygate.

A Claygate old people's social outing, 1955. Their coach is photographed outside The Hare and Hounds, Claygate Green, Claygate.

The 206 London Transport bus service photographed in Hare Lane, Claygate, sometime in the 1970s. The Claygate Resident's Association fought a campaign for a through bus service to Kingston upon Thames in the late 1970s. Surrey County Council and London Transport agreed to replace the existing 206 bus service with a more direct 215 service from Claygate to Kingston upon Thames. The new service came into operation on the morning of 28 October 1978.

A photograph of Mr C. N. Hibbert riding a motorcycle and sidecar combination with his daughter-in-law, Mrs H. Hibbert, seated behind him and his own daughter, Mrs B. Crundall, sitting in the sidecar. This picture was taken in the summer of 1923 on The Green, Claygate. Mrs Crundall is holding her baby daughter, Joan, who was born earlier that year. Mr H. Hibbert, son of C. N. Hibbert, was a professional landscape gardener and for many years often worked abroad on large contracts. During the First World War he was working south of Paris and according to his son, Charles H. Hibbert, could hear gunfire from the fighting on the Western Front. He was called up into the Army in 1915 and served until 1921. The Hibbert family ran a fruiterer's and grocer's business from a shop opposite The Green from 1915 until it was finally closed in November 1995 by Charles Hibbert. The building to the right of the motorcycle is a tithe barn which was demolished shortly before the outbreak of the Second World War; the iron railings were cut up for scrap metal and never replaced.

Mr Charles Hibbert serving a customer in his shop in 1991.

Mr Charlie Hainsworth, a Claygate butcher's delivery boy, poses on the box seat of his pony and trap for the photographer, c. 1913.

Two photographs of the building of the Esher bypass, now known as the A3, taken in October 1974, near Claygate. Esher residents had campaigned for a bypass for many years, in an attempt to divert traffic away from the Portsmouth Road. Traffic congestion in Esher increased once the Kingston bypass was opened in 1928, and by the 1960s the Portsmouth Road was regularly blocked by traffic jams. Eventually the Government agreed to build a bypass, which became part of the A3 London to Portsmouth road.

This is a lovely photograph with which to finish this book as it illustrates the rural life of the area nearly 100 years ago. It shows The Old Cottage, Claygate Common, and was photographed in about 1910. Actually it is a photograph of Copseham Cottage used by George Meredith, the Victorian novelist-poet. Meredith was a great lover of nature. He first lived at The Limes in Weybridge from 1848 until 1853 when he went to live at Fairholme in Esher. He later left there in 1858 and moved out to Copseham Cottage. Meredith was inspired by the flora and fauna of the area. *Robin Redbreast* and his novel *Richard Feveral* were written while he lived there. Meredith stayed at Copseham Cottage until 1864 when he left to live at Kingston Lodge, Kingston upon Thames, where he wrote *Vittoria*. Copseham Cottage survived until the 1960s in private ownership. Later, it was demolished to make way for the Esher bypass.

INDEX

SWANSEA AT WAR

SALLY BOWLER